Women Putting A Stop To All The Drama

I0416395

Written By:

Shevaughna Sweat

Women Putting A Stop To All The Drama
By: Shevaughna Sweat
ISBN: 978-1-4116-0519-0
Copyright 2013
All Rights Reserved
Published By Lulu

*In the loving memory of Triska LaShaun Rose,
Briana Roshae Roberson, and Mya Lanay Love*

A Message from Sister to Sister

You made me laugh, whenever I was sad
You encouraged me when I was having a bad day
Thanks for listening to me and the encouraging words
That you shared along the way

You helped nurse me back to health
When I was feeling a little bit under the weather
As we all know we must go down this road
I know that we will walk around Heaven someday together

There were some who envied our relationship
But they could not relate to the storms that we had to face
They don't even realize that without bearing the cross
You will not be rewarded your crown in Heaven
When you reach that higher place

I have an assignment from God
That you know that I must fulfill
We will definitely see each other again
According to the Master's will

We both struggled as a single parent
The depth of our struggle only God knows
I present this poem to you, my sister
I LOVE YOU, with all my heart Ms.Triska LaShaun Rose.

To My Loving Girls

A love one is a treasure of the heart
And to lose one is like losing my heart.
I lost Three beautiful girls that I wanted to keep forever with me.
The Lord knows my loss is so great;
Suddenly acceptance is required and no permission is asked.
I will treasure my memories now and remember the times we shared.

Shaun, loved the Lord and her church.
She is such a caring, thoughtful, generous person, always willing to help.
My baby was quick to quote scriptures and to discuss the word

Briana (Punkie), my beautiful oldest grand-daughter just entering the eleventh grade, A Brigade dancer and Team Aspiring Singer.
I will miss the young woman you were becoming.

Mya (Dough Baby), You are the love of my life, an Honor Roll student with a swift response and a million dollar smile.
Mya, would have made a great politician!

I will cling to my memories and hope that one day that I heal.
My babies did not die, they slept away.
Until we meet again,

Love Momma & Memaw

To my daughter, Briana Roberson

You are my princess; I cared for you so much
I looked at you when you were born and the innocence you brought to my heart.
That is something that will be taken away from me.
No suffering or tragedy, no deeply seeded pain
could ever over shadow the bond that we retain
Remember, I am you daddy and yours to keep
I am going to miss you dearly!
I love you from the deep down in my heart

Love Always,
Daddy

Do The Right Thing

Watching people die
Seeing people's death
In such violent ways
I'll never forget

Violent thugs
Selling drugs
Beating women
Shooting, stealing

Crack Cocaine
Weed and Wet
Selling drugs to addicts
That struggle to quit

Now I'm done talking
I've done all I can do
Police stop the violence
And you can, too

Written By: Jamesia Lockley

Preface:

At some point in life women can avoid some of the unnecessary drama we are faced with. I know that it is not just me. Do you sometimes get that gut feeling or soft voice saying, "Don't do that?" Especially when you think about being tempted to get yourself involved in certain situations? And for some reason, you ignore it! Unfortunately weeks, months, or maybe years later, you always find yourself saying, "I should have followed my first mind."

Table of Contents

I know quite a few mothers have gone down this road at sometime or another with the baby daddy drama. Although sometimes women can avoid some of the chaos they put themselves through.

Think about this scenario. You meet a guy, you go out with him a couple of times, and now you are ready to take the relationship to the next level. First of all, you need to get to know this man. Ask questions!! While you are still dating, the man never mentions anything about church, but he brings up the subject of sex. Duh! Hello! Sex is his first priority. He will only care about pleasing himself.

(Matthew 5:28) But I say to you ever a man that looks on a woman to lust for her has already committed adultery with her in his heart.

If you look closely, you can see his horns and the pointy tail. Girl, you're flirting with Satan himself. (You're so gullible; you get goose bumps just because your new man called you "Baby".) Go online to see if he's married, or if you reside in Houston go to the Family Law Center, because he's not going to tell you that he is married. See if he will be upfront about all of his past relationships, kids, or if he was married, what happened to cause their marriage to end in divorce. If he has children make sure he's paying child support. If he's not, what could this man possibly do for you? If he would stoop low enough to neglect his own flesh and blood, then he will not care too much about you, either. So don't you foolishly get *pregnant with a child for a man who has neglected the children he already has! Men are supposed to be formed in the image of God! The Lord never neglects us, and we are all His children. So I guess these men think that they can neglect their children and get away from taking care of their children, financially and emotionally. Just because the parents are not together, the children should not have to suffer! I believe the parents should have the children's best interest and just let the past be history.*

Well, I will not put all the blame on the men. There are some women who have plotted and schemed to trap a man by saying that they are pregnant, when they really were not. On another note, they really don't know who is the father of the child. In this regard you told Michael that you are pregnant for him, but you were with Leroy 3 days before Michael, and with Andre a week before Leroy. (I guess you called Cleo an asked her who is the father of your child.) That's sad! Keep in mind if you point the finger at someone, there are most definitely three fingers are pointing right back at yourself!

Ladies, the child support is for the kids. It is not for you to go shopping for yourself, or to get your hair and nails done. I know too many women who spend all the child support on themselves. They go shopping and buy themselves an outfit to wear to the club, and then they go get their hair and nails done. Every time you see them, they are dressed from head to toe, and the child/children are wearing the same clothes over and over. Okay, let's say that your children are with their father. It is his weekend to have the kids. Every time he has them, he has to take them shopping. He probably will not mind, out of love for his children, and will not say anything to the children. (But in the back of his mind he will wonder what she is doing with the child support checks.) I would not spend my kid's money on myself. I actually show their daddy the receipts and the items, just so he can never say I'm spending the kid's money on myself. I would buy their clothes and put mine in layaway.

For the sake of everyone, if the relationship is over, then just walk away. (Why would you scratch up his car with some sharp object, slash his tires, break his windows, or put sugar in the gas tank? You drive by his house to see if another woman is over there. You go to the man's job, causing a scene, now the man is forced to file for a restraining order against you. Is it worth all of the drama? Are you going to achieve the goal that you are striving so hard to conquer? Why try to keep a man, who obviously does not love you?) Why is it that if a man has children, he always goes by himself to pick them up? (If you are going to be a part of his life, then why can't you go with him to pick up or drop off the children, unless he is still fooling around with the children's mother?) Don't play house with the father of your children after the children have gone to bed. The children should not be caught in the middle, because the father is angry with you and will not spend time with the kids, or you're angry with him and won't let him see the kids. Whatever the situation may be, don't let that cause the father of the child to start to totally neglect the children, or if he is currently paying child support then he will suddenly stop.

I'm a single parent myself, and I am so tired of these deadbeat fathers. There are a lot of men who want children and their wives can't have children. Some of the men, who have children, do not care to be a part of the children's lives. These men will quit one job and find another job and they will not report the new employment information. It should be made legal for the custodial parent to obtain the current job information needed to file a court ordered child support case, and address on the absent parent. That will stop a lot of chaos! What happen to the real men? Are they all up in heaven with the Lord? The deadbeat dads make the fathers who are paying child support suffer.

Ladies, know where your children are at all times! In this day and time, girls and boys are being sexually molested, kidnapped, brutally beaten, and some even murdered. Don't be overwhelmed with the new man in your life, and then you start to neglect your children. The man will not be around long, but your children will still be there! All you are worried about is that the child/children are gone for the weekend, and you are ready to party, go out of town, going to the casino or the clubs and getting your groove on! Don't let your kids go to any and everybody's house. Please, take the time to get to know the parents of your kid's friends. You should find out who their friends are, if their friends are being raised in a respectful home, or if they have some habits that may influence you child to experiment with sex, crime with gangs, drugs, or alcohol. Teenagers hormones are running wild, and they are pressured to explore different things, especially while in high school. How do you know if your daughter is truly at her friend Lisa's house, and not pretending to stay the weekend over a friend house to meet a boy from school, who happens to live right across the street from Lisa?

{Keep in mind when your teenage daughter or son starts lying to you, don't get mad because they learned it from you. I know that you are saying, how did I teach my child not to tell me the truth. Okay, I will tell you the Easter bunny, the Tooth Fairy, and Santa Claus. These are traditional lies. Easter is about the resurrection of Christ, not a rabbit. Jesus went to Calvary and he died on the cross for your sins and mine so that we may have eternal life, and that is the celebration of Easter Sunday. Okay, don't forget about the Tooth Fairy. In this day and time if we notice anyone or anything strange in our houses, we will either call the police or grab some type of weapon. And last but not least, Santa Claus. The only one man that knows every boy/girl's, man /woman's name, and whether they have been bad or good is the Almighty God. So don't teach your children to have faith in make-believe characters. Teach them to have faith in God, because He is the only one who will never leave nor forsake them.}

The kids in middle school are sexually active in

in these days! I don't know about you but I don't want to be a grandmother at an early age! Make the sacrifice and talk to your daughters! Don't let them find out the information on the streets and from fellow students, that they should have learned the dos and don'ts from you. Let them know that they don't have to be pressured into doing something they are not ready for. There would be a lot less single parent homes if we as women would concentrate on only one man, the only man, the Almighty God. He is the only man that will never forsake you. He most definitely will take care of you, and supply all of your needs. He is always right by your side. You never have to worry about him cheating on you. He is the only man that women will not mind sharing. Men come and they go! But it's up to you to decide not to be another notch in a man's belt. Don't worry about pleasing any man, but the Lord!

(1 Corinthians 7:34) An unmarried woman should spend time with the Lord and be focused on how to please the Lord.

Chapter 2:
Having Respect for Yourself

I encourage all women to take a reality check, every once in a while! There are some women who have very low self-esteem. You must learn to love yourself before anyone else can love you. Yes, there are quite a few women who think that the outer appearance makes the person. They feel if you don't dress a certain way, look a certain way, buy all the expensive name brand clothes/shoes, drive a certain car, live in a certain house in a certain neighborhood, make a certain salary, etc., then you are considered a nobody. That's definitely not true! I am my Father's child and He is the ruler of all the earth, so that makes me a queen.

Ladies, you do not have to dress in skimpy clothing to feel good about yourself. Speaking for myself, I feel like a million bucks in a pair of jeans, a nice casual shirt and some comfortable shoes. Some women dress like that to attract a man; others do this for different reasons. If you happen to meet a nice guy and you're dressed half naked, then what will be left for his imagination? Somewhere out there you are being closely watched by someone who looks up to you. Especially those of you who have daughters! If they see you dressed in sleezy clothes, then they will want to dress like that, too. Dressing this way brings about the wrong attention!

I guess when men see women dressed this way, they feel that these women don't respect themselves, so they won't respect you either! Men will feel as if they can say, touch, or do whatever may pop up in their wicked minds. (For Example: The Texas Beach Party in Galveston, TX every year) I have never been to these gatherings, but I have heard and seen pictures of the chaos that takes place. Women walking around in bikini and thong swimsuits for attention. (Just to see how many numbers they can get.)

Oh yes, it has gotten the wrong attention! A host of one-night stands, divorces and other torn relationships. It also brings about many unwanted pregnancies, forced intercourse (rape), and many STD's. At a function like this if you do meet a guy, trust me, he has collected many different phone numbers. Keep in mind a lot of people who attend this party reserve hotel rooms in advance, and the majority of the guests are men!

There are those women who have no respect at all for themselves or anyone else. They will actually go to church dressed in provocative attire, wearing short skirts, skimpy low cut blouses, halters or dresses with the back out showing their tattoos. (The guy's name in the tattoo left you high and dry years ago.) In that frame of mind they didn't come to church to hear the word of GOD.

(Leviticus 19:28) You shall not make any cuts in your body for the dead, nor make any tattoo marks on yourselves: I am the Lord.

(1 Timothy 2:9) And I want all women to be modest in their appearance.

I want all women to adorn themselves with proper clothing (modestly and discreetly), not with braided hair or gold or pearls or showing off expensive clothing, but with good deeds, appropriate for women who profess to worship God.

I know that the Bible says come as you are, but I don't think it was meant for the clothes you would wear to a club.

(1 Peter 3:3-4) And let not your adornment be merely external: braiding the hair, and wearing gold jewelry, or putting on dresses; but let it be the hidden person of the heart, with the imperishable quality of a gentle and quiet spirit, which is precious in the sight of God.

Chapter 3:
A Lesson Learned

I must say to those of you who fall in this category, "Don't let anybody use you!" There are quite a few women who will take care of a man, just to say that they have a man. Some have such low self-esteem. They feel as though they want to hold on to the man that they have, because they feel that no other man would want them. When you meet the man, make sure that he's working on a steady job (I mean a legitimate job with health, dental, 401K and vision benefits, not a street pharmacist.) If he's not working when you meet him, then 9 times out of 10, he's not trying to find a job. (Girl, you can do bad all by yourself.) But on the other hand, if he's laid off, within a couple of weeks to a month, he should be back on another job. A real man will take care of his responsibilities.

(1 Timothy 5:8) But if anyone does not provide for his own, and especially those of his household, he has been denied the faith, and is worse than an unbeliever.

He would be too ashamed to leech off the woman that he's dating. A real man will not want to drop you off at work so that he can drive your car, and then go back home chilling in the A/C, watching cable, and eating up groceries your hard earned money has bought. First, and foremost when you leave for work in the morning, he needs to be leaving also, going in the opposite direction to his own job, in his own vehicle. If he can't pay the car note, fill the gas tank up, keep it clean, and stay updated on all of the maintenance on it, then he can't drive the vehicle. I have known women who didn't think twice about the idea of a man dropping them off at work, until he picks them up late, or doesn't pick them up at all. Or, is it a case where one of your friends saw your man driving some other woman around (with the sunroof open) in your car? Most of the time people don't take care of your belongings like they would their own. Some people don't care about anyone, but themselves! They tend to drive recklessly or have many unpaid parking or traffic tickets in your car and with no intention of telling you about the tickets until your car has been impounded. (Drama)

I must hang out for a minute right here, to talk to the single women. First of all, you can't trust everybody with your heart. They will only use your heart as a doormat. Some of you have been in relationships for years, and you feel since you have invested so much of your time in that relationship then you may as well hang in there. You may think that you will eventually win this guy's heart so that maybe he will marry you someday.

[Okay, there is a lesson to be learned!]

I must say thanks to the creator of LOONEY TUNES. Watch, because you will miss the point I'm trying to make! (The Roadrunner and Wild E. Coyote, we all have watched this show for many years.) Now the coyote has done everything he could think of to catch this bird, but he has failed. The coyote has experienced disaster after disaster trying to catch this bird. And that is the way some of your relationships have been, or maybe the one that you are presently in you're going through drama. You have done everything that crosses your mind, but the man still has no plans to spend the rest of his life with you as his wife, not a live-in girlfriend. (You make sure your family has clean clothes, cook the food, and keep the house clean, you are faithful to him, you plan romantic things for the two of you to do, and you have children together.) The children are not going to keep the man, so stop using that excuse! You have been going through drama for years, trying to please this man. The Lord has been trying to get your attention for years, He has put many obstacles right in front of you, but you ignore it. You grew up in the church, now that you are grown you make excuses not to go to church. And you ask the question, why you can't find a good man. I am a living witness that Mr. Right will find you, if you stop trying to hook yourself up, and let God bless you.

By all means, please don't get caught up in things that are very material. I know plenty of women who want $250,000.00 houses, the finest cars, and wear nothing but the best clothes. If your salary (not your boyfriend's, fiancé's or husband's) is not in the hundred thousands, then you don't need to try to live above your means. How are you going to live like the Banks family on The Fresh Prince of Bellaire when you only have the finances of the Evans family on Good Times? If you want the finer things in life get off your blessed assurance, work hard, and buy them yourself. Ladies pay your own bills, rent, credit cards, *insurance, etc,. How were you paying your bills before the man came into your life?*

Don't use anybody and you will not be used either. Remember, you will reap whatever you sow! And I dare not leave out the part about women who only date athletes, policemen, some ministers, and men in the military making a certain salary, driving a certain car, and living in a big house in a certain neighborhood. Some men that fall in each category mentioned can not be trustworthy.

{I have the perfect example: Two of my friends were dating two guys that went to the military. They would call frequently, write letters, and visit the military bases to spend time with their boyfriends. They thought they were in love. The two guys had completed their military assignments and they both came back with unusual souvenirs. (Their wives) They failed to tell these two women that they had encountered a relationship while on duty. If they are not married, they meet women in every city that they have traveled to. Some of the men know ahead of time that some women are very materialistic.}

(James 2:1-4) My brethren, do not hold your faith in our glorious Lord Jesus Christ with an attitude of personal favoritism. For If a man comes in to your assembly with a gold ring and dressed in fine clothes, and a poor man in dirty clothes, and you pay special attention to the one who is wearing the fine clothes, you say to the rich man "You sit here in a good place", but you say to the

poor man, "You stand over here or sit down by my footstool." Have you not made distinctions among yourselves, and become judges with evil motives?

I want you to think about this scenario for a moment. Suppose you are out and about with your girlfriends and along come this guy driving a regular car (Let's say a 1988 Chevy truck,) wearing some jeans, a casual shirt, and some comfortable shoes. As he approaches, he says hello, you and all your girls speak to this man, but all of you quickly return to the somewhat shallow conversation that was already in discussion. (Of course that subject was about which man you would let buy you a drink. But only if he looked like he was financially stable.) As he approaches one woman who is sitting alone at a table, they introduce themselves and that is when a friendly conversation started. The conversation they had eventually led into a steady cozy relationship and then on to marriage. It comes to find out that the next time you see this man; he's filthy rich, lives in a four or five bedroom house, has two or three cars (that are paid in full), and last but not least, a wife (The same lady that looked beyond what he was wearing or what he was driving and accepted him for who he was and not his money).

It all boils down to not judging people for the way they are dressed, the way they look, the kind of car they drive, or anything else under the materialistic nature. By the way the truck was not his. It belonged to a friend. He just wanted to keep a very positive outlook that he could meet at least one woman who would be interested in him and not his money. Let that be a lesson not to be judgmental! (This old is a true statement... Never judge a book by its cover.)

Women Stop Hating On Other Women

Why do some people still have hang-ups about interracial relationships?

You have a problem with seeing a black man with a White, Hispanic, or Asian woman. (Or maybe a Hispanic man with a Black, White, Asian, Indian, or whatever the case may be.) You have no idea who God destined you to be with! God loves us (no matter what color the skin is), and sent His only begotten son to die for all of our sins. This means He gave His life for you and me. So who are we to have hatred against other races? What makes one race better than the others? I do not have a problem with interracial relationships. According to genetics, we all are mixed interracially somewhere down the line. You have to be happy for you, not for your family, friends or the rest of the world. I was taught to look at a person for who they are, not the color of his or her skin. If people are still having a problem with other races, that is just a sign of prejudice and immaturity. Mentally they have not grown.

(James 2:8-9) If however, you are fulfilling the royal law according to the Scripture, "You shall love thy neighbor as yourself," you are doing well. But if you show partiality, you are committing sin and are convicted be the law as transgressors.

On the other hand, it all boils down to pure jealousy. Why can't we celebrate with our fellow sister when they receive a blessing?

(Exodus 20:17) You shall not covet thy neighbor's house, spouse, or anything that belongs to your neighbor.

She has a man and you don't. You have not had a man since the man help reproduce you some years ago. You walk around all frowned up, looking down your nose at people. That's why you don't have a man now! Be patient and wait on your blessing. The negative attitude you have toward certain situations can block many of your blessings. Be happy for your neighbor, when it's your turn you will want everybody to be happy for you.

Ladies, why do you get angry when you see a woman who wears a size 3, the size that you were way back in the day, before you had any kids? It is not her fault that you have gained weight and upscaled to a size 24. If you want to lose the weight, then do something about it. Do some exercise! Walk around the track at a steady pace or you can jog. Stop complaining that you can't lose the weight especially when you are sitting in front of the television eating a Mrs. Bairds' glazed honey bun after midnight. Limit yourself to the daily amounts of cheeseburgers, hot dogs, breads, pizza, juice (sugar sweetened) soda, starches, cakes, pies, cookies, and candy that you eat. Try some of these items: baked chicken or fish, a baked potato, fruit salad, or tossed green salad (no salad dressing). The salad dressings are supposed to be fat-free, but they really contain a lot of salt. Drink plenty of water! (8 glasses a day is required) Stay focused and be encouraged!!!

You have nothing to lose, but to shed some unwanted pounds.

Ladies, those of you who are mothers and have sons let your children grow to be responsible young adults! Stop causing all the friction in their lives and marriages. In the Bible it says, that a man shall leave his mother and father and cleave unto his wife. How will he ever do that if you are still treating him like a baby? You can't hold his hand and pacify him forever. And on the other hand you want him to be with someone that you picked for him to be with. You have lived your life, now let him live his. You try every scheme in the book to try to break up his relationship. (For example: You are always borrowing money all the time, dropping by frequently and unannounced, or insults on the down low.) Let's say that you succeed; now you are happy, but your son is depressed and sleeping in your guest bedroom. If it is meant for the two of them to be together, they will reconcile and you will be labeled as the "Meddling Mother-In-Law". The same thing goes for your daughters let them make their own decisions, unless there is some domestic violence involved in your daughter's relationship. No one is perfect, except the Almighty King JESUS. Mistakes will be made. We live and learn from our mistakes. If he's not the one that God chose for her, eventually she will see that he is just Mr. Right Now. She has to be the one to say enough is enough.

When God created you, He created a genuine masterpiece. So, why are you always trying to be like someone else? Each time that you see your best friend, she just came from shopping at the mall. Your best friend is single, with no children, lives by herself, never been married, and faithfully pays her tithes. She can afford to shop whenever she feels like shopping. You, on the other hand are a single parent with three kids, living from paycheck to paycheck to make ends meet and refuse to make the sacrifice to pay your tithe. You are separated from your husband and living with another man. Whatever she does, you go right behind her and try to do the same thing, but a little better. You are trying to compete with her, but now you don't have enough money to pay your bills that are due next week. Life is not a competition!

Chapter: 5
Strongly Against Abuse

I will reach a subject that some women may have had an experience with that brings tears to my eyes, and that is DOMESTIC VIOLENCE!

By any means necessary do not accept abuse of any kind whether: physical, verbal, mental, and that also includes sexual. There are no exceptions; rape is still a crime, even if you're married!! If the relationship starts out this way, then he is not the man for you.

Women were put on this earth to be a mate to a man and to be loved unconditionally. Not to be treated as a punching bag. In my views, all the discipline that you didn't receive from your parents teaching you right from wrong throughout your childhood years, then you don't need to receive from no one else other than the Almighty God!

It reminds me of the passage, spare the rod; spoil the child. And my mother didn't spare any rods! (But let me clarify discipline: You know the times you were told not to do certain things, but you did them anyway. You were told to do your household chores by the time your parents came back, but you were on the phone, playing video games, gone outside, or just doing whatever you wanted to do and not what you were told to do.) All these things you either caught a whipping, or you were punished. You couldn't talk on the phone, play any video games), you couldn't go anywhere (to school and back, and to church on Sundays.) And you were told, don't ask for *anything except breakfast, lunch and dinner. I'm not the only one who heard the words, don't ask for nothing because I'm not buying nothing. As I said you were taught discipline by your parents as a child. No woman deserves to be treated like an animal, walking around with black eyes, bruises, bloody noses, busted lips, broken arms/legs, rape, and even death. It's sad to say, but some women are treated this way for years. Some feel that it's their fault, but it's not! He will act like this to be controlling, and to scare the woman. He may apologize, and promise to never do it again. That's just another lie!*

I'm quite sure every woman in America has seen the movie "What's Love Got To Do With It". Tina eventually got tired of Ike punching her around, she started punching him back. In my opinion, Tina waited too long. She should have taboed him the first time he hit her. If you don't let these men know ahead of time what you will not tolerate, and that is specifically DO NOT EVER RAISE YOUR HAND TO HIT ME BECAUSE THERE WILL DEFINITELY BE SOME CONSEQUENCES and mean every word! It should not take for a woman to be hospitalized or worse because these men can't control their anger, or is it that they may have watched their father treat their mother this way. That's not love! It's against the law, it is a crime, and it should be reported.

I have talked with several people and they revealed how domestic violence has affected their life, by a family member, a friend, or a co-worker. I would like to share their thoughts.

The heart of a mother

I put an end to mine when I saw the fear in my daughter's eyes. Seeing her so frightened gave me the inner strength to do the right thing. I didn't want my child to grow up thinking that is how men are supposed to treat women. If one cannot make a change for themselves, then do it for the child. The children are our future. We have to give them the tools to learn to survive in the world.

S.H.

Encouraging One Another

In my opinion, as far as rape victims are concerned, women dressing in moderate attire would be the first step. Just because an item is sold in the stores it does not mean you have to wear it in public. Some of the dresses, skirts and shorts are so short if the wind blew slightly then you may catch a cold. Some man out there will be enticed by some of the outfits that are worn. Why bring negative attention to yourself?

V.R.

You are somebody!!

Domestic violence can be stopped. First of all, one must have the inner strength to over come. When a man puts his hands on a woman it's either because he's on a power trip, or he is it that he's very insecure. Domestic violence starts in the mind. They make you feel less of a person, like you cannot make it without them. You were alive and well and a lot happier before you met this man. You don't need a man to survive, especially one who will abuse you. If you don't believe in yourself, then no one else will either. There is a hero inside you. Hopefully there are no children involved. They can pick up those same patterns, the weakness or the need to empower others. In order to stop violence, you must start with yourself. Once you realize that you are somebody and deserve better, then you will do better.

N.H .

There are also two other forms of abuse, such as mental and verbal abuse. Mental abuse for example would be: him telling you that you are ugly, saying that you need to lose some weight, saying that nobody else wants you, or telling you that you will never amount to anything. Verbal abuse would be: him calling you profane names, calling you stupid or some of the other hurtful names. Ladies, you do not have to accept this type if behavior from any man. God gave us the strength to survive any obstacle. He created you to be a helpmate to a man; it just may not be the man that you chose to be with. When God brings you your designated mate, you will not go through all of this drama.

Love does not hurt! If a man truly loves you he would not do anything to intentionally hurt you. Be patient and wait on God for a God-fearing man!

Single Women

All women are queens in their own eyesight. We are gifts from GOD to be a mate to a man. These are not my words, they are written in the bible.

(1 Corinthians 11:8-9) For man does not originate for woman, but woman for man; for indeed man was not created for woman's sake, but woman for man's sake.

Now for that matter, it doesn't mean you be a mate to (Tom, Harry, Larry, Michael, and so on….) It means that you are chosen to be with one man that the LORD has designated you to be with, not some other woman's husband, fiancé, or boyfriend. Until you finally settle down and live righteously, you are pushing your own blessings further and further back.

Some women are so desperate to have a man that you are willing to stab a close friend or relative in the back by sleeping with their husband, fiancé, or boyfriend. You don't take the time to think about how that friend or relative will feel when they find out what you have done. You don't have a man, so you don't care about anyone else. Two friends of mine say that they have experienced the ultimate unforgivable act. (The wife in one situation, and a girlfriend in the other situation, slept with one of their own flesh and blood cousin. They both knew that they were related and they just didn't care.) Both of them need to be put in a padded cell, because that is sick! If you are not in a relationship with your designated mate that God chose for you, then you are setting yourself up for chaos that can really be avoided!

Think about this!!

I know quite a few women who have complained about how they are not being satisfied intimately in their relationships. The man talks a great deal about the skills he has when it comes to lovemaking. However, he turned out to be the Chief Executive Operator in the Minute-Maid Dept. (Okay maybe some of you didn't catch that.) The encounter lasted only five minutes. He used to be a Sugar Daddy, but now he's just a Milk Dud. (Okay, I was really thinking California Raisin.)

(2 Peter 2:17-19) They are like dried up springs of water or as clouds blown away by the wind promising much, but delivering nothing. They are doomed to blackest darkness. They brag about themselves with empty foolish boasting. With lustful desire as their bait, they lure back into sin those who have escaped from such wicked living.

God created intimacy to be pleasurable between a man and a woman. God created intimacy for **married** couples. If he is not the man that God designated you to be with, he's the one that you settled for. If you are not married you should not worry about pleasing yourself and the world, you should focus on pleasing God. I know a lot of women who want the storybook fairytale marriages. But how will you ever have the perfect love if you are too impatient to wait on GOD to bless you with the mate that he has chosen for you?

Wait patiently for your mate, he will find you! Don't you go looking for a husband! (Putting an ad in the personals, subscribing to the dating services, chatting online, having one night stands with guys that you meet at the club, or a blind date set up by a friend or relative.)

Remember, it is in the book of **Proverbs 18:22 "He that findeth a wife findeth a good thing**. It doesn't say, She that findeth a husband….

I don't know about all of you, but I want to be loved just as JESUS loves the church!! I will not say that I want to be loved, as a man loves his own body!! Because that is not true for all men in this society. If he loved himself, he wouldn't live eating out of fast-food restaurants, drinking alcohol, smoking cigarettes, doing drugs, and going from woman to woman after woman….

Fast foods are greasy and they can cause ulcers or clog your arteries. Alcoholic beverages can cause liver and other internal damage. Cigarettes cause cancer and they are bad for your lungs and heart. A warning label is written on the box. They are hazardous to your health.) Drugs can be fatal! And some STD's you can take an antibiotic to treat. But AIDS is not a joke! It is real and fatal!

Dating

You may ask yourself why you're going through the drama of his cell phone ringing excessively. Girl, I'll tell you why, because he has turned the ringer off on the house phone, so you won't answer the phone when his other women call. Think about this: You can't answer his phone now when it rings!! Remember what's done in the dark will eventually come to light. Okay, but you're sitting right next to him, so who is calling him? You will probably get a response like, "Oh, that's just my homeboy John-John!" And you know that you have met all of his friends, so why won't he answer the phone? Drama!

You wonder why the man has not proposed yet. If he has not mentioned the subject of marriage after the two of you have been dating for a while, then he's not going to. It does not take years for a man to know if he wants you to be a part of his life.

Let's say the two of you go to the mall, if he leads you into the jewelry store, okay he will get an "E" for effort. But keep your eyes open, to see if he leads you straight to the rings on sale. The ring cost $999, but it is on sale for 70% off. Girl, he only loves you 30%. The diamond is so small, that you need a magnifying glass and the eyepiece that most custom professional jewelers use. I am quite sure that you have met some men who would be rather cheap about it and buy you a ring from a pawnshop. Is that all you are worth to him, second hand products? We serve a first-class God, so that means we should not settle for leftovers or second best. I am not saying that he should go into the marriage in debt, but getting married is a sacred occasion and the rings should show a symbol of his love for you.) Maybe you will get a ring, but sit back and relax to see if he's ready and willing to set a wedding date. When a man really loves a woman, he will be ready to commit. There would be no excuse or delay of the actual wedding ceremony.

Dating exclusively, and a little bit extra

Many women are still in the same train of thought by having what they call a spare tire or sidekick while they are supposed to be in a relationship. If you break up with your steady boyfriend, then you have someone else you can call on a rebound. You are running from man to man. Let me explain: You are in a relationship with a guy that you say that you really love, and he treats you like a queen but the intimacy has gone downhill. Now you have started to reject this man but since you have invested so much time into the relationship, you would rather not leave, and you do not want to see him with another woman. You do not want the man, but you don't want anybody else to have him either. You are selfish and greedy. Then there is the "Sugar Daddy". The man who wines and dines you, who takes you shopping, pays your bills, and the intimacy is a 12+ on a scale of 1 to 10. That just goes to show you were already looking for a downfall in the relationship, and it also shows that you are very insecure. You are afraid of being by yourself.

*Take a minute to relax and be by yourself for a while! Take time to spend with the Lord. Don't be one of those women who only mention the Lord when someone has mistreated you. You are quick to say that "God don't like ugly." How do you know what God likes? You never devote any of your time to be in the presence of the Lord. You might go to church twice a year (**Easter and Mother's Day**).*

Shacking Up

Well, I know I'm going to step on a few toes in this chapter. So I will just say "OUCH" for you! Please stop shacking up and playing house!!

(1 Corinthians 7:8-9) But I say to the unmarried and to widows that it is good for them to remain even as I. But if they do not have self-control, let them marry, for it is better to marry than to burn.

You are already giving the man everything in a relationship, except the marriage license and a ring on your finger. If he is compassionate and a God-fearing Christian man, then he will think of the consequences that both of you will face by living together. A lot of relationships end in turmoil because many women marry or get engaged to a man that is unequally yoked. You are at church on a Sunday and he's at home with some of his best friends: Imported Beers, Budweiser or Bud Light, Johnnie Walker (Red/Black), Old "E", Heineken, Colt 45, or Mad Dog (20/20). A family that prays together stays together. What makes you think that he would marry you when you're giving him husband benefits?

Being The Other Woman

Here is something to really stop and think about:

Have you ever cheated in one of your past relationships, or have you been involved with a married man before? Maybe you didn't know he was married. Look at his hands; look for the ring around the finger. (Not the gold band, but where he has taken the ring off and left it in the glove box of his car or truck.) Let's take it a little further. Have you ever caused a relationship to fall apart? Keep in mind if you break up a relationship to get with this man, and now you are with him, why would you think your relationship with him will be happily ever after? Eventually, the tables will turn and there goes the drama.

There are some women who don't mind being the other woman. There are some ladies that throw themselves at men just for a good time. (Yes, I'm talking about intimately.) They are only interested in getting a quick thrill. Too many women settle for less than God's best. You know upfront that you are willingly breaking two of the Ten Commandments:

(Exodus 20: 14 and 17) Thou shall not commit adultery. (No cheating allowed.) Thou shall not covet anything that belongs to thy neighbor. *(For example: a spouse, a car, a house, children, and etc.)*

They seem to like that the man has to go home, and they don't have to worry about seeing him again until one of the two makes a phone call. Some women believe the lies that men tell them: "Oh, I'm only there for the sake of my child/children" (the other lie), or "I'm in the process of getting a divorce", or "All she wants to do is argue and nag me all the time". Well, maybe she wouldn't nag you if you show her that she's appreciated and made time for your family and not always out with the boys. Especially, if those homeboys are not married.

(1 Corinthians 13:11) When I was a child, I spake as a child, I understood as a child, I thought as a child, But when I became a man, I put away childish things.

(Ex: You outgrow the things you did as a child.)

Married

I'm not through yet! Don't think for a second that your man can do no wrong, and will not cheat on you. Girl those are the ones you can't let your guard down with too quick. It doesn't matter if he may come straight home after work. He very well could be a 9am to 5pm adulterer. Some men could have everything that they look for in their wives, but yet they still cheat. Don't be cheesing too much because he brings you flowers. There is such a thing called a "guilt gift". How do you know that he didn't get a 2 for 1 special at the flower shop, and just because he's feeling a little bit guilty, you're the lucky winner of that extra bouquet? He starts to call you every hour on the hour, it's not always because he loves you. It very well could be because he wants to know your whereabouts before he does his dirt, chasing every thing in a skirt. And that's a scary thought!!

In this day and time you can't tell the men from the women or vice versa! The women are dressing and acting like men and the men are dressing and acting like women. Ughhh!! That's enough to make you nauseated. Some 7-Up and saltine crackers are needed right now.

Men dating men. Women dating women.

What has the world come to? GOD created a woman for man, not a man for man nor a woman for woman. Adam and Eve, not Adam and Steve nor Betty and Eve. (That's disgusting and a sin!)

(Genesis 2:18) It is not good that the man should be alone; I will make him a help mate for him.

(Leviticus 18:22) You shall not lie with a man as you do with a woman, it is abomination.

(Leviticus 20:13) If there is a man who lies with another man as he does with a woman, both have committed a detestable act; they shall surely be put to death. Their blood guiltiness is upon them.

And likewise for the women who have mated with other women.

If you suspect that he's cheating, 9 times out of 10, he is!

Here are a few facts to look for:
*1.) I have to work late. (**Oldest lie in the book**)*
2.) He walks in the door with an attitude, picks an argument with you, just so he can find a reason to leave again.
*3.) You notice that he's trying new positions or moves on you that he tried with her or them. (**The intimacy is really short. When you first got married, it was 2 or 3 hours, now it's only 2 or 3 minutes**.) It's something wrong with that picture! That's just another lie about to ooze out his mouth. You may get a response like, "I don't know what's wrong!" Um Huh!!*
4.) New underwear that you have never seen before, because you buy all of his personal items of that nature. (T-shirts, underwear/boxers, socks, etc.)
*5.) He might say to you that "It's not you, it's me!" He may also say "I need my space." Let me tell you what that's all about. He wants to see other people. He has found a new female that he wants to play with for a moment. He will continue to keep in touch with you, just in case the grass in not greener on the other side he wants to keep the lines of communication open with you. And you will know if it is not greener on the other side, out of the blue he will start wanting to spend more time with you. (**He will drop by your house unannounced, he will call to see if you have plans for lunch or dinner, or he will even start to get a little bit jealous of your friends who happen to be men.**)*

6.) He comes home at 3, 4, 5 o'clock in the morning. (You haven't talked to him a ll day. He really expects you to believe that he's been hanging out with the homeboys all night long.) {Back in the day, any two ways that I stay out all night, and I have not talked to my significant other, you already know that I have not been out all night long with a bunch of women.} Come on tell the truth and shame the devil!

*7.) He accuses you of cheating on him. His guilt is shifted off on you.(**Dead giveaway**)*

*8.) If you know that you do all the shopping, and you buy Zest soap, why does he come home smelling like Irish Spring or Coast (**The Eye-Opener)?***

9.) His text messages and call logs deleted on his phone, phone on vibrate, or a secret phone.

These are definitely true statements! I saw the majority of these in my mother's marriage, and that's how I knew a bold-faced lie when I heard one in my own marriage.

If you happen to be married and either of you cheat then you just don't love that person, so walk away. I have to be real and say that it's not just the men. Ladies, don't try to throw stones and then hide your hands. Ladies, there are some devious women out there! Misery loves company! As long as they get what they want, their happy. To show you that this statement is true, have you ever noticed the most destructive hurricanes and tropical storms have been named after women? Hmm!! I'll just let that marinate for a minute!

Ladies don't clap too loud, don't be on the telephone or have your girlfriends over all the time. Is the person really your friend or hanging around you to get to your man? You never really can tell! I'm not saying that you have to spend all of your time with your spouse, but don't neglect him either. Marriage is a sacrifice on both parts, and it's 100% give and take, not 50/50.

Married, but separated

I know a lot of people who are married, but separated. They have been married for 20 years and separated 19 of the 20 years. Why would you prolong an issue for that long? If there are no kids involved, and no unresolved feelings between either of you, then why are you procrastinating with moving on with your life? You might hear the woman saying: "Well he left me", then he should file for a divorce. Or, you might hear the man saying: "Well she left me", then she should be the one to file. I know it may be a money issue, nobody wants to pay the attorney's fee, or court costs. Here's the solution for that: go to the library and tell the clerk that you are interested in finding the book that is entitled, "How to Do Your Own Divorce." Trust me, the cost is much cheaper than paying an attorney.

As I conclude this chapter, I pray that you take the words of wisdom to heart. When you finally meet that special man, you are engaged, and about to be married, make sure that you are ready, as well as your fiancé. The vows are sacred and they should be taken very seriously and not be broken by the husband or wife under any circumstance. God honors marriage. As I said before, marriage should be 100% give and take by both husband and wife. Make sure that you are marrying for the right reasons: you love each other unconditionally, and want to build a life together. Do not marry for the money, how the person looks, how good they may be intimately, or revenge toward someone from a past relationship. It is better to marry for character and not for emotions. I know someone who married out of spite toward someone, and his marriage lasted a little over two months. He even tried a third time but that marriage ended in divorce also. It will not always be peaches and cream. I can guarantee there will definitely be some disagreements! Marriage is hard work, but if there are two people willing to work together then it is definitely worth the sacrifice.

(Ephesians 4:26) Be angry and yet do not sin; do not let the sun go down on your anger.

You should never go to sleep at night with unresolved anger. This will not only interrupt a good night's sleep, but one of you may not wake up the next morning, or one of you may leave for work and something fatal may happen. The disagreement was probably something petty and not worth the energy of being upset with each other. You will never be able to apologize and tell them how much you love them. I hope that these inspirational words have helped you in your next relationship. **Thank you and God bless you!**

Special Bonus:

Wise Words To Live By

*Life has its struggles
And some storms are often hard
You will make it through
As long as you are being obedient to the will of the
Lord*

*Don't be hoaxed into a one night stand
Because you will have to face that hardship alone
Raising a child by yourself,
Living in a single-parent home*

*He may call you a female dog or a garden tool
But know your worth which is far above a ruby, a
precious jewel*

*Don't subscribe to the dating websites
That is not the plan we were created to do
Patience is a virtue, so be encouraged
And wait for God to bless you*

*As a Virtuous woman
I don't have to tell you to take a stand
Don't settle for less than God's best
To be an appetizer for any man*

*He's sampling over here, and sampling over there
He has sampled any and everywhere
Society says it is the thing to do
But what happens when he finds out some young
man has treated his daughter the same way he
treated you*

Ladies, avoid at all cost
Getting involved with a married man allowing him to
come and go
If he's cheating on her with you
Eventually you will reap exactly what you sow

It was God's idea
That man shall not live by bread alone
So don't fret how you have been treated by your ex
Because God sits high and looks low from upon his
throne